D0459072

CALGARY PUBLIC LIBRARY

JUL   2010

NEW YORK CITY

Richard Platt

Illustrated by Manuela Cappon

KINGFISHER

NEW YORK

New York City

On a map of the United States, you have to search around for the city of New York. It is tucked away on the right, in a corner of the state with the same name. But in reality, New York City is difficult to miss. It is a city that is big in every way. It is even visible from space—for at night, New York City glows brighter than anywhere else on the East Coast.

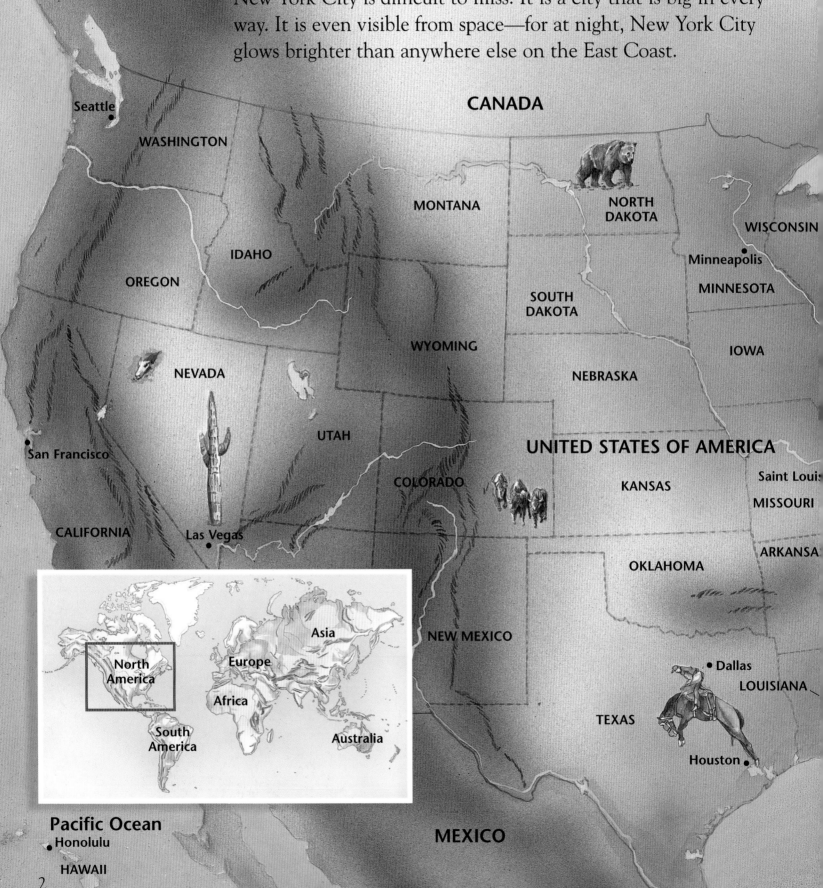

CANADA

Seattle

WASHINGTON

MONTANA

NORTH DAKOTA

WISCONSIN

IDAHO

Minneapolis

OREGON

MINNESOTA

SOUTH DAKOTA

WYOMING

IOWA

NEVADA

NEBRASKA

San Francisco

UTAH

UNITED STATES OF AMERICA

COLORADO

KANSAS

Saint Louis

MISSOURI

CALIFORNIA

Las Vegas

ARKANSAS

OKLAHOMA

Asia

Europe

North America

NEW MEXICO

Africa

Dallas

LOUISIANA

South America

Australia

TEXAS

Houston

Pacific Ocean

MEXICO

Honolulu

HAWAII

2

But New York City was not always so large and vibrant. Compared with other famous cities in the world, it is a very young one. In 1600, when London, England; Damascus, Syria; and Beijing, China, were already ancient, the New York area was still forests and fields. But the city grew up fast. In the 400 years that followed, New York has crammed in a lot of history. And what a history!

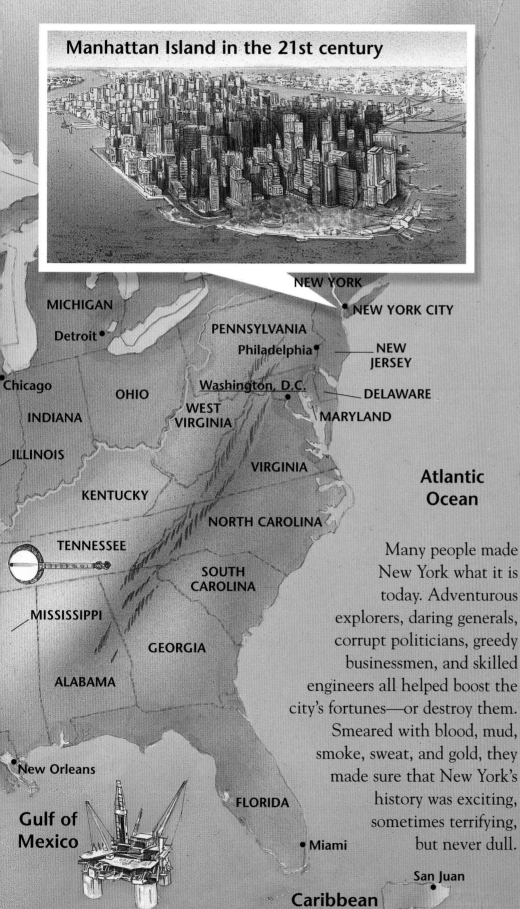

Manhattan Island in the 21st century

NEW YORK

NEW YORK CITY

MICHIGAN

Detroit

PENNSYLVANIA

Philadelphia

NEW JERSEY

Chicago

OHIO

Washington, D.C.

DELAWARE

INDIANA

WEST VIRGINIA

MARYLAND

ILLINOIS

VIRGINIA

Atlantic Ocean

KENTUCKY

NORTH CAROLINA

TENNESSEE

SOUTH CAROLINA

MISSISSIPPI

GEORGIA

ALABAMA

New Orleans

FLORIDA

Gulf of Mexico

Miami

San Juan

Caribbean islands

Many people made New York what it is today. Adventurous explorers, daring generals, corrupt politicians, greedy businessmen, and skilled engineers all helped boost the city's fortunes—or destroy them. Smeared with blood, mud, smoke, sweat, and gold, they made sure that New York's history was exciting, sometimes terrifying, but never dull.

New York timeline

20,000 B.C. Frosty glaciers cover America's northeast coast.

3500 B.C. Native American people begin to settle in the area around the river that we now call the Hudson.

A.D. 1600 Delaware people are living on Manahatouh, now called Manhattan.

A.D. 1609 English explorer Henry Hudson visits the river valley on a Dutch ship called the *Half Moon*.

A.D. 1614 The Dutch claim the region. They call it New Netherland and start the Dutch West India Company to develop and settle it.

A.D. 1623 Dutch settlers start to build New Amsterdam, a fortified town at the tip of Manhattan Island.

A.D. 1664 Fed up with Dutch rule, New Amsterdam's people welcome invading English soldiers, who rename the town New York.

A.D. 1720 New York is a busy port, grown rich from trading sugar with the Caribbean islands to the south.

A.D. 1776 Along with other Americans, New York's citizens reject rule from England. The American Revolution lasts from 1775 to 1783.

A.D. 1820 Immigrants swell New York City's population, making it the busiest port in the United States.

A.D. 1856 Work begins on a huge new public park in central Manhattan.

A.D. 1863 A protest against fighting in the American Civil War turns into a violent race riot.

A.D. 1883 Brooklyn Bridge, the world's longest, opens. It spans the East River.

A.D. 1886 The French people give the Statue of Liberty to New York.

A.D. 1892 There is now a center, on Ellis Island, to process the immigrants flooding in from Europe.

A.D. 1907 The New York City Subway (underground train system) opens.

A.D. 1929 New Yorkers who gambled on the stock market lose everything in the Wall Street Crash.

A.D. 1939 In Queens, the World's Fair opens. In Europe, World War II begins.

A.D. 1950 The new United Nations building makes New York one of the most important international cities.

A.D. 1962 An exhibition by the painter Andy Warhol launches pop art.

A.D. 1969 New York welcomes Apollo astronauts returning from the Moon.

A.D. 2001 9/11 disaster: terrorists fly planes into two New York skyscrapers.

A.D. 2006 Construction begins to replace buildings destroyed in the 9/11 attack.

What do these dates mean?
B.C. means "before Christ." For example, 100 B.C. refers to 100 years before the birth of Jesus Christ, as traditionally calculated.

A.D. means "anno Domini" (medieval Latin for "year of our Lord") and refers to all dates after the birth of Christ.

20,000 B.C.

A.D. 1500

A.D. 1700

A.D. 1800

A.D. 1900

A.D. 2000

Contents

As you turn the pages of this book, you will unravel the full story of New York City. You will meet the people who have lived there and watch as they build and rebuild this exciting, restless place. Even the name of the city has changed over the years, but perhaps it will always be known by its nickname—the city that never sleeps.

Business beehive
page 18

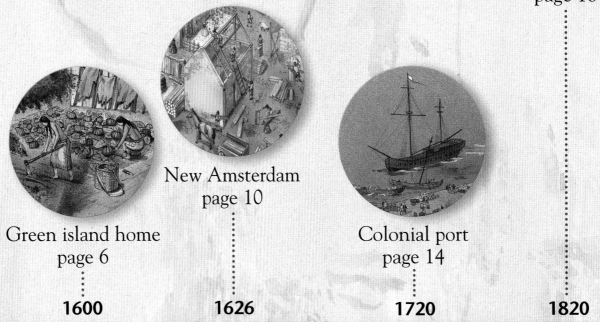

Green island home
page 6

New Amsterdam
page 10

Colonial port
page 14

1600   **1626**   **1720**   **1820**

1609   **1664**   **1776**

The English
take over
page 12

New York City in 1906

N

New Jersey

Central Park

Old Delaware settlement

Hudson River

East River

Brooklyn Bridge

City Hall

Broadway

Brooklyn

Ellis Island

Liberty Island

Governor's Island

A locator map shows how the city is growing over time and where each scene takes place.

Hudson
visits
page 8

Revolution!
page 16

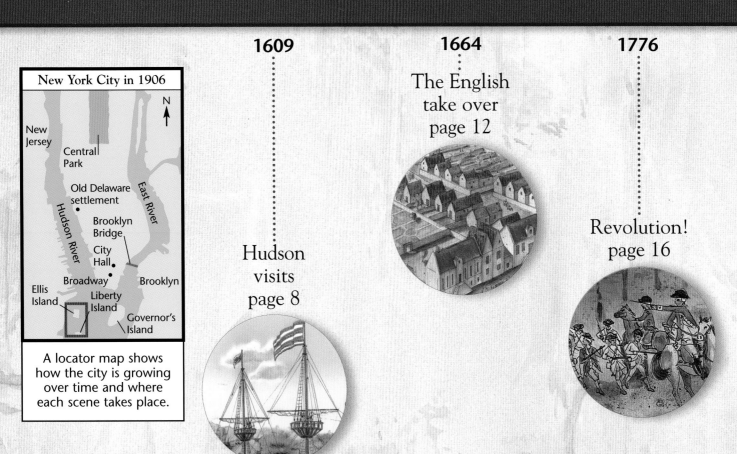

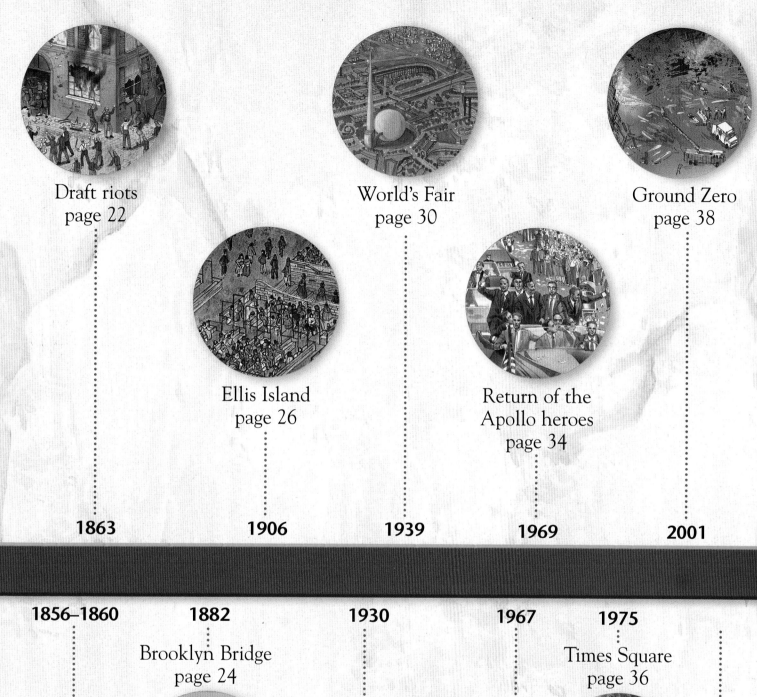

1863   **1906**   **1939**   **1969**   **2001**

1856–1860   **1882**   **1930**   **1967**   **1975**

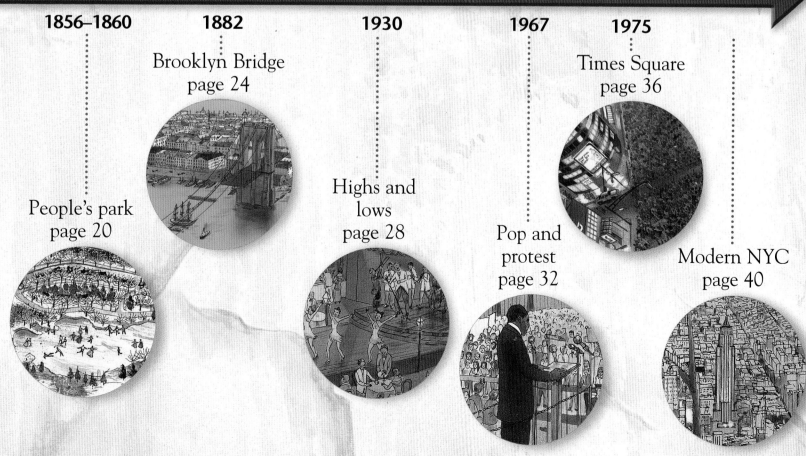

Green island home 1600

In a huge bay, a tree-trunk canoe glides across the choppy water. The two canoeists dip their paddles rhythmically into the river to steer the craft. They are heading toward their home, located on a lush, wooded island they call "Manahatouh." A basket between them overflows with twitching fish. Cleaned and grilled, they will make a delicious supper for the family.

These Native American people are the Delaware, also called the Lenape. Their ancestors settled in the area we now call New York City about 6,000 years earlier. They fished its deep, cold rivers, hunted the plentiful game, and collected seeds, roots, and nuts. Over time, they felled some of the trees that covered Manahatouh and farmed the open land.

Potters shape long snakes of clay into thin-walled cooking and storage vessels.

raccoon hunts provide both meat and fur

raccoon

women use hoes made from branches and stone blades to dig the fields

making stone tools

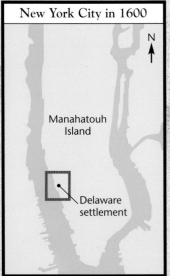

New York City in 1600

N

Manahatouh Island

Delaware settlement

Delaware women tend the small gardens, growing crops that add variety to their meals.

sharper than steel, the stone blades make quick work of skinning and cutting up fish

the harbor and creeks provide the community with rich meals of shellfish

For money, the Delaware use "wampum": drilled shell beads on thread or woven into belts.

fishermen use baskets to scoop up oysters

felling trees to create new fields

dogs help on hunts

a huntsman with a bow and arrows

fences protect a sacred graveyard

tree bark on a wooden frame creates a cozy house for one or more families

maize and tobacco crops

weaving basket containers to collect and protect food

local clay provides material for cooking and storage pots

weaving wampum

a baby is bound to a cradleboard to keep it safe and comfortable

a fire dries and preserves fish, meat, and animal skins

dogs are also spirit guardians—when they die, some are buried in decorated graves

a canoe is made by burning away the wood inside a large log

fishermen paddle far from their camp to find the best catch

the rivers and creeks provide a speedy transportation network for the canoeists

Now, in 1600, the waterside camp is busy with activity. The people who live here are skilled craftworkers and traders. They make pots and baskets. Women sew clothes from animal skins. Men chop and burn trees to make canoes. The Delaware people are healthy and fit. They are rarely hungry. Their wooden homes keep them dry. Fires warm them in the winter. What more could they possibly want?

Hudson visits 1609

One day in the late summer, a giant sea monster appears in the bay. To the Delaware people, its round body seems bigger than a thousand canoes. Small, square clouds billow above it, pulling it along. Men scurry busily upon its back. At first, only the most curious and brave of the Delaware paddle out to take a closer look at the beast.

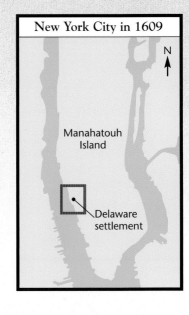

New York City in 1609

N

Manahatouh Island

Delaware settlement

in the mouths of the Dutch sailors, the word "Manahatouh" becomes "Manhattan"

to the Dutchmen, the carefully tended Delaware settlement looks like a crude camp in an untamed wilderness

the deep water around Manahatouh allows the *Half Moon* to sail fairly close to the shoreline

inquisitive Delaware people paddle out to the *Half Moon* from their camps on Manahatouh

The Delaware people are eager to trade for metal tools because their own stone blades break easily.

used to a diet of dried and salted food, the Dutch sailors drool over the fresh fruit and meat that the Delaware bring to trade

During an earlier skirmish with local people, one of Hudson's crew was shot through the neck.

The "monster" is actually a ship from the Netherlands, the *Half Moon*. Its English captain, Henry Hudson, is seeking a way to sail from the Atlantic Ocean to the Pacific Ocean. From Manahatouh, Hudson follows a "great river to the north" but turns back when it becomes too shallow to sail any farther. The river will later be named in his honor.

the relaxed lifestyle of the Delaware people seems "lazy" to Hudson's crew, who are used to lives of grinding hard work

the Manahatouh air smells sweet to the ship's crew after months at sea in a cramped, crowded ship

crew members climb the rigging to adjust the sails when the wind changes or when coming toward the shore

Although Hudson is disappointed, his visit has not been a complete failure. He is amazed by the beauty of the new land that he has discovered and by its abundant fish, game, and fruit. The *Half Moon*'s crew trade with the Delaware, swapping beads and metal tools for fresh food, tobacco, and for something altogether more valuable—animal furs. Hudson knows that Europeans will return for the furs alone.

when they are hoisted, the huge, square sails catch the wind, making sailing ships the fastest way to travel long distances

Henry Hudson (c. 1565–1611) could not interest English merchants in his voyage, so he sailed for the Dutch instead.

the Dutch flag flies from the stern (rear)

"whipstaff" mechanism operates the rudder, to steer the ship

the *Half Moon*

rudder

barrels and boxes in the hold contained enough food and drinking water for the two-month ocean crossing

the sides of the *Half Moon* tower above the canoes like a wooden wall

New Amsterdam 1626

Henry Hudson's voyage causes a sensation. The Dutch government claims the land that he has discovered, calling it "New Netherland." Wealthy merchants start the Dutch West India Company to exploit its riches—especially the valuable beaver furs. Returning to Manhattan, the company builds a fort at its tip to guard the rivers on either side.

the town windmill grinds grain to make bread flour

The Dutch pay for Manhattan with goods worth 60 guilders, the same as a laborer's yearly earnings.

army barracks

Fort Amsterdam is actually a relatively poorly protected stockade, with crude earth and log walls

cannons on the ramparts

Dutch flag

repairs to the fort's earth wall

the main road, *De Heere Straet*, leads north from the waterfront

pigs roam freely, foraging in the muddy streets for food

a merchant ship moored at the great dock, loaded up with valuable furs to take back to Europe

Company officials want to legally "buy" Manhattan. The Delaware people who live here are used to doing deals. Families regularly trade hunting rights with neighbors. But in their eyes, land—like air and water—is for all to enjoy. They do not understand the idea of owning it. So they "sell" the island very cheaply, accepting a bag of tools and trinkets for it.

New York City in 1626

N

Manhattan Island

Old Delaware settlement

Hudson River

East River

Beaver fur is valuable for its warmth, and the animals have been hunted almost to extinction in Europe.

Dutch ship sailing down the Hudson River, returning from the north with animal furs

only the grandest buildings are built from bricks and tiles, transported from the Netherlands

Manhattan's new "owners" waste no time. Around the fort, they lay out streets. Carpenters build houses from rough-sawn planks. A few finer buildings, made from stone and imported Dutch bricks, rise up along the waterfront. More settlers arrive to plant crops and raise animals. Before long, they have made a town that reminds them of their Dutch homeland. They name it after the Dutch capital: New Amsterdam.

the governor lives in a fancy house within the stockade

church

beyond this settled area, Manhattan is still covered by swamp and forest

taverns provide the settlers with entertainment, home-brewed ale and imported gin

strips of farmland

Using only long handsaws, cutting trees into long planks is exhausting work.

houses made from sawn planks and roofed with reeds

building timber from felled trees

a stone counting house, or bank

the warehouses of the Dutch West India Company line the waterfront

craftsmen work with simple hand tools

The English take over 1664

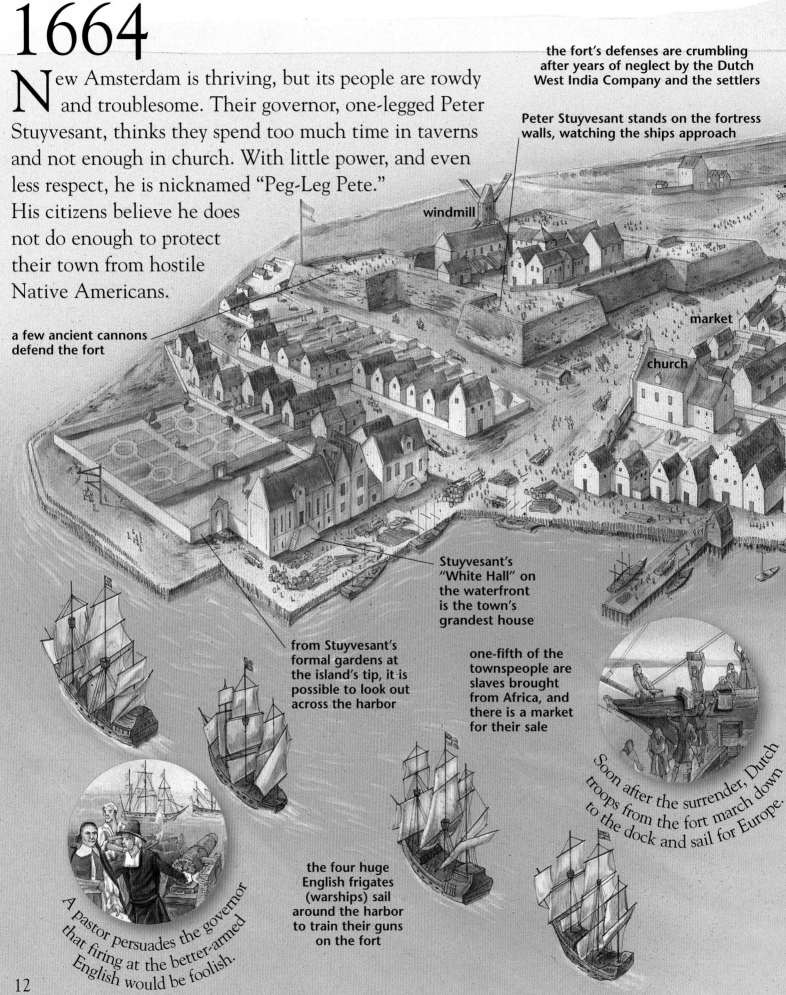

New Amsterdam is thriving, but its people are rowdy and troublesome. Their governor, one-legged Peter Stuyvesant, thinks they spend too much time in taverns and not enough in church. With little power, and even less respect, he is nicknamed "Peg-Leg Pete." His citizens believe he does not do enough to protect their town from hostile Native Americans.

the fort's defenses are crumbling after years of neglect by the Dutch West India Company and the settlers

Peter Stuyvesant stands on the fortress walls, watching the ships approach

windmill

a few ancient cannons defend the fort

market

church

Stuyvesant's "White Hall" on the waterfront is the town's grandest house

from Stuyvesant's formal gardens at the island's tip, it is possible to look out across the harbor

one-fifth of the townspeople are slaves brought from Africa, and there is a market for their sale

Soon after the surrender, Dutch troops from the fort march down to the dock and sail for Europe.

A pastor persuades the governor that firing at the better-armed English would be foolish.

the four huge English frigates (warships) sail around the harbor to train their guns on the fort

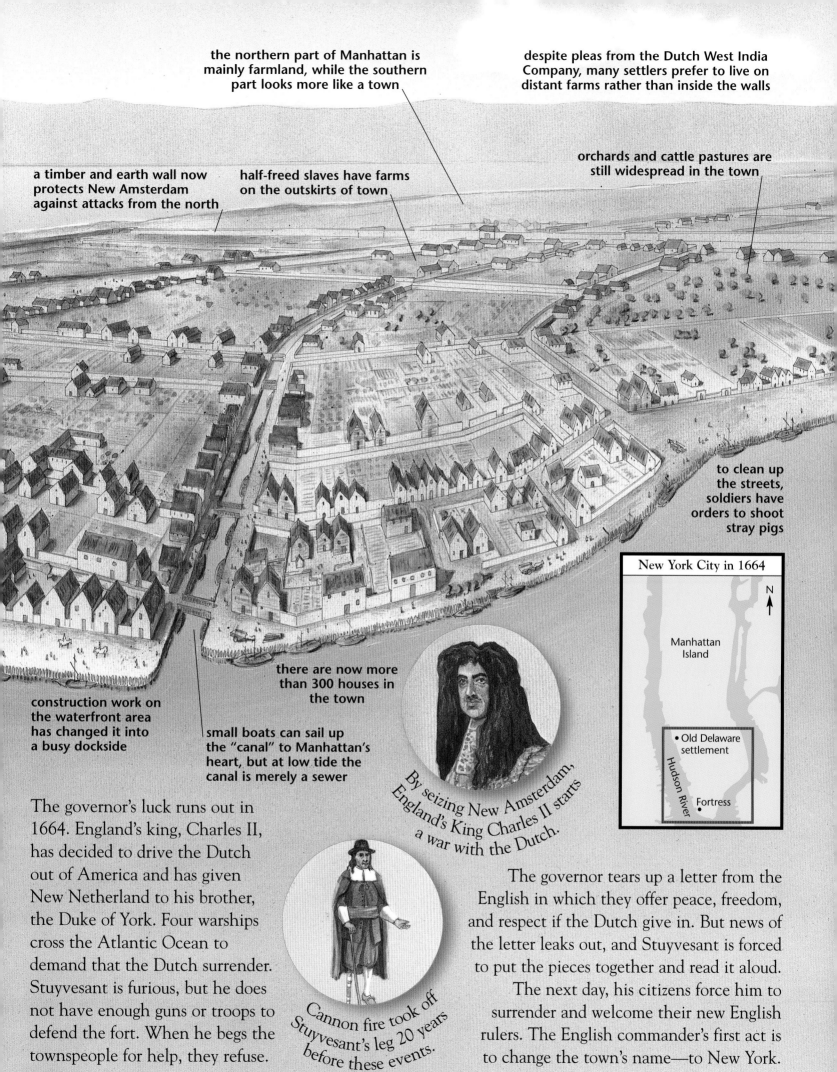

the northern part of Manhattan is mainly farmland, while the southern part looks more like a town

despite pleas from the Dutch West India Company, many settlers prefer to live on distant farms rather than inside the walls

a timber and earth wall now protects New Amsterdam against attacks from the north

half-freed slaves have farms on the outskirts of town

orchards and cattle pastures are still widespread in the town

to clean up the streets, soldiers have orders to shoot stray pigs

New York City in 1664

N

Manhattan Island

Old Delaware settlement

Hudson River

Fortress

there are now more than 300 houses in the town

By seizing New Amsterdam, England's King Charles II starts a war with the Dutch.

construction work on the waterfront area has changed it into a busy dockside

small boats can sail up the "canal" to Manhattan's heart, but at low tide the canal is merely a sewer

Cannon fire took off Stuyvesant's leg 20 years before these events.

The governor's luck runs out in 1664. England's king, Charles II, has decided to drive the Dutch out of America and has given New Netherland to his brother, the Duke of York. Four warships cross the Atlantic Ocean to demand that the Dutch surrender. Stuyvesant is furious, but he does not have enough guns or troops to defend the fort. When he begs the townspeople for help, they refuse.

The governor tears up a letter from the English in which they offer peace, freedom, and respect if the Dutch give in. But news of the letter leaks out, and Stuyvesant is forced to put the pieces together and read it aloud.

The next day, his citizens force him to surrender and welcome their new English rulers. The English commander's first act is to change the town's name—to New York.

Colonial port 1720

Business is brisk in the crowded streets around New York's harbor. Thanks to thriving trade, the city's merchants have grown rich and powerful. Their ships carry food and timber to Caribbean islands and return loaded with coarse brown sugar. Refined into sweet white crystals or turned into rum, it fetches high prices in England.

This profitable trade has made New York a boom town. Mills sift flour for export. A warehouse grinds tobacco leaves into snuff—a fine dust for sniffing. New ships are under construction on riverside wharves. Taverns do a roaring trade as thirsty sailors roll in with every tide. Even Manhattan itself is growing as workers reclaim land to push back the East River.

But there is also a sinister side to the town. One-sixth of New York's people are slaves, who are bought and sold like cattle. Shady smugglers land illegal cargoes without paying dock taxes. At night, thieves haunt the unlit, stinking streets. New York is now a city divided between wealthy merchants and downtrodden workers. It is a tense community, with poor, enslaved laborers everywhere.

Smugglers secretly unload their cargoes before docking, to avoid New York's customs taxes.

dumping rubble inside a wall of wooden stakes reclaims land from the river

chandlers sell everything sailors need to stock and repair their ships

sly merchants are experts at avoiding import taxes

a dockside tavern

cobblers make and repair shoes

sugar refinery

Heating sugar in water and mixing it with "spice" (bullock's blood) makes the crystals whiter.

drying the sugar

purifying the sugar

without water power, mills have to rely on horses to turn machinery

this mill grinds barley, to be used in brewing beer

brown, unrefined sugar fills the holds of ships from the Caribbean

African slaves, traded on ships in the harbor, are in big demand for New York's most unpleasant tasks.

merchant ships are moored so densely that their masts make the East River look like a forest

exchange building

bakery

New York's main streets run parallel to the two great rivers

fashionable English gentlemen wear showy outfits

coopers make barrels for storing cargo on long sea voyages

New York City in 1720

N

Manhattan Island

Old Delaware settlement

Hudson River

East River

Revolution! 1776

The people of New York, as well as their neighbors who are also part of the Thirteen Colonies, have nobody to represent them in the British Parliament. However, they must still obey Parliament's laws. So when their British rulers demand higher taxes on sugar, tea, glass, paper, and even playing cards, the Americans refuse to pay. Their rebellion sparks a war.

The Declaration of Independence, signed four weeks before the battle, asserted U.S. freedom from British rule.

nine American soldiers retreat toward Gowanus Creek, where they drown while crossing a bridge that has been destroyed by mistake

The defeated Americans surrender to the German Hessian soldiers rather than give in to the British.

fusillades (muskets fired together) make up for the guns' lack of accuracy

American Commander George Washington is the last to retreat across the foggy East River.

sharp bayonets turn guns into deadly swords for hand-to-hand fighting

the American troops attack across low, muddy farmland

the muskets used by both sides are inaccurate—they cannot hit a target more than 300 ft. (90m) away

400 Maryland troops fight to capture the stone house

New York City in 1776

N

East River

Manhattan Island

Brooklyn Heights

Brooklyn

In 1776, the American colonies vow that they will rule themselves and sign the Declaration of Independence. The British response is to attack New York. A huge fleet of British warships crosses the Atlantic Ocean, carrying 32,000 well-drilled troops. Their American foes are mostly amateurs. Outnumbered and out-gunned, they clash with the British at Brooklyn Heights on August 27.

Defeat comes swiftly. American troops flee across the East River to Manhattan. Disheartened and disorganized, they make easy targets—until a squad of soldiers from Maryland leaps to their defense. Charging time after time across swamp and river, they hold off the invaders. Their bravery saves the lives of many of their comrades. The Marylanders will help drive out the British over the next five years.

a stone house provides the British troops with valuable cover

2,000 Hessian mercenaries (hired German soldiers), in blue uniforms, back up the British attack

the Hessians are very disciplined and have modern weapons

Victory gives the British control of New York, but a fire destroys one-fourth of the city just days later.

musketeers (gunmen) fire from the windows of the stone house

British "Red Coat" soldiers

the tennis ball–size iron balls, shot from the cannons, are terrifying but not very accurate

after each shot, the muskets need to be reloaded

though they fight bravely, the American soldiers cannot defeat the British

even the quickest soldier can fire only three shots per minute

Business beehive 1820

As the 1800s begin, New York City is not the capital of the newly formed United States of America—that is Washington, D.C. Nor is it the biggest city in the country—that is Philadelphia. But no other place can rival New York's importance. It is simply the brightest, brashest, richest, loudest, fastest city on the continent.

City Hall, completed in 1812, was expensive to build, so only the front of it was finished in marble.

huge ships, which would run aground in other ports, can moor safely on the Hudson

wharves now line the Hudson River, as well as the East River

Hudson River

the grand marble front of City Hall faces the old town

the world's first steam ferry service leaves from a wharf on the Hudson River

steam ferry wharf

the fashionable stores on Broadway do not yet have big display windows

built four years earlier, Castle Clinton defends Manhattan from attacks

the cheap backside of City Hall, made of brownstone, faces new streets

the city's financial center is on Wall Street—a street that follows the old Dutch wall

in Lower Manhattan, the older streets still trace the shoreline

thanks to its busy harbor, New York will soon be bigger than Philadelphia

Broadway

A politician, a surveyor, and a lawyer plan the new streets, ignoring hills and other obstacles.

The world's biggest ships can moor in the deep-water harbor, to load goods for export to hungry European markets. New York is now a financial center, too, with major banks and a stock exchange. As migrants and merchants flock to the city, property prices soar. Hemmed in by water on three sides, the city expands quickly in the only direction it can: to the north.

a very wealthy one-fifth of New York's citizens own four-fifths of the land in the city

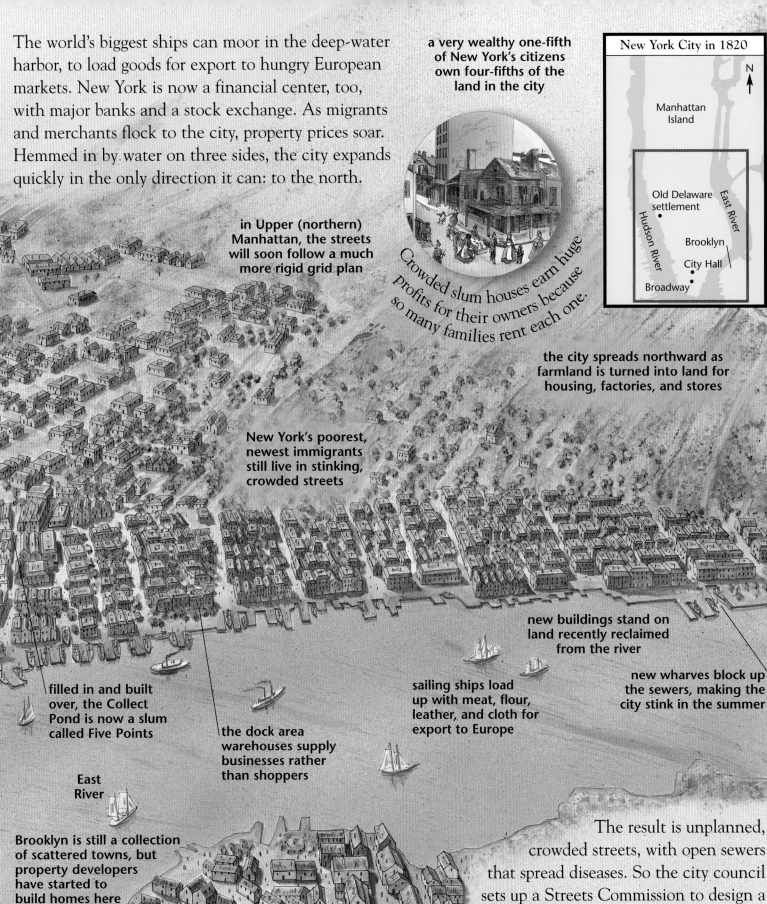

New York City in 1820

N

Manhattan Island

Old Delaware settlement

East River

Brooklyn

Hudson River

City Hall

Broadway

Crowded slum houses earn huge profits for their owners because so many families rent each one.

in Upper (northern) Manhattan, the streets will soon follow a much more rigid grid plan

the city spreads northward as farmland is turned into land for housing, factories, and stores

New York's poorest, newest immigrants still live in stinking, crowded streets

new buildings stand on land recently reclaimed from the river

filled in and built over, the Collect Pond is now a slum called Five Points

sailing ships load up with meat, flour, leather, and cloth for export to Europe

new wharves block up the sewers, making the city stink in the summer

the dock area warehouses supply businesses rather than shoppers

East River

Brooklyn is still a collection of scattered towns, but property developers have started to build homes here

The result is unplanned, crowded streets, with open sewers that spread diseases. So the city council sets up a Streets Commission to design a "new" city. In 1811, the Commissioners' Plan is ready. It sets out a pattern of wide avenues running north and south and numbered streets running east to west, up to the docks along the shore. It also states that all new buildings must be cleaner, lighter, and healthier.

19

some of the land chosen for the park is wilderness

tenants who rent houses on the land are made homeless

grand park buildings include two-story homes

only the poorest residents live in shacks and shanties

Seneca Village is completely wiped away by the clearance of land

workers fell trees and clear poison ivy

masons building bridges cost far more than planned

workers break up rocks to make road materials

surveyors measure land heights and areas

The park's planners wanted it to be a mix of country landscapes and more formal walkways.

Summer 1856: clearing the land

Fall 1858: construction in progress

These New Yorkers, made jobless by a business slowdown, are fighting for work on the park.

People's park 1856–1860

Manhattan's problems grow despite the grid plan. Poor New Yorkers are still packed into airless, unhealthy slums. The rich complain that—unlike London and Paris—New York lacks open green spaces where they can drive and ride. In 1848, a landscape architect named Andrew Downing suggests a solution to both problems: a gigantic park.

New York City in 1860

N

Central Park

Old Delaware settlement

Hudson River

East River

Brooklyn

City Hall

Broadway

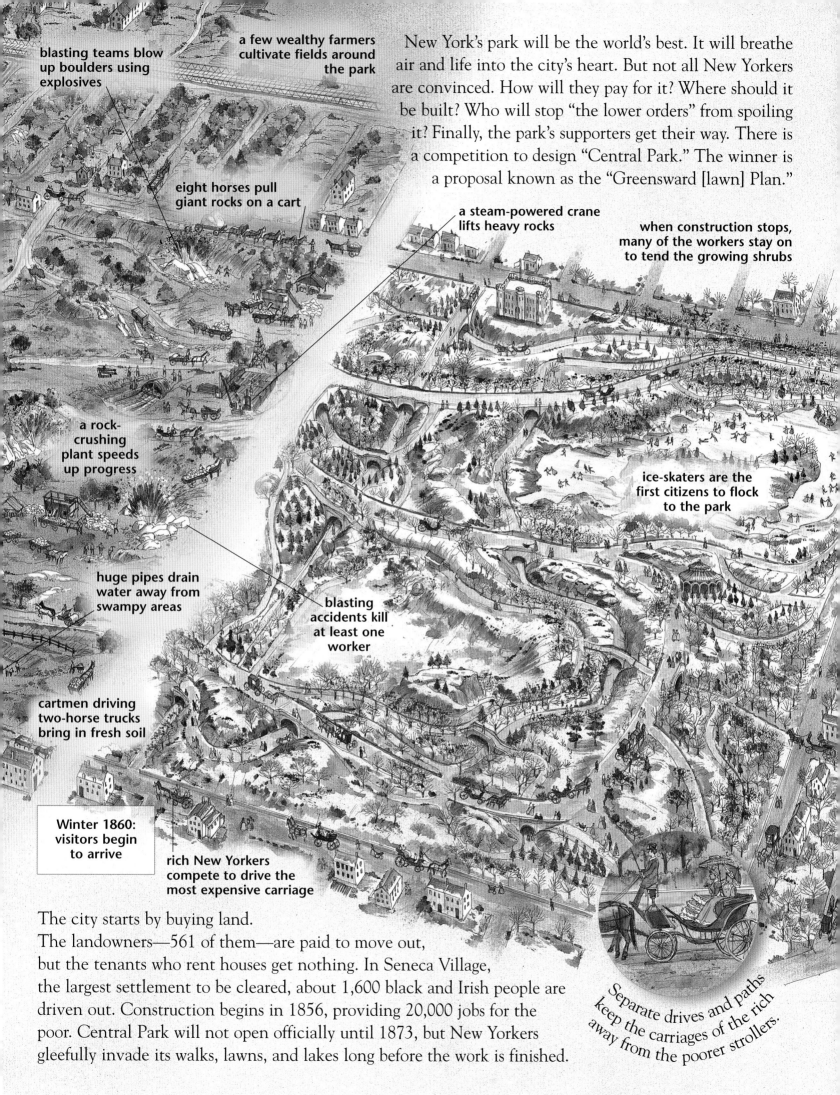

blasting teams blow up boulders using explosives

a few wealthy farmers cultivate fields around the park

eight horses pull giant rocks on a cart

a steam-powered crane lifts heavy rocks

when construction stops, many of the workers stay on to tend the growing shrubs

New York's park will be the world's best. It will breathe air and life into the city's heart. But not all New Yorkers are convinced. How will they pay for it? Where should it be built? Who will stop "the lower orders" from spoiling it? Finally, the park's supporters get their way. There is a competition to design "Central Park." The winner is a proposal known as the "Greensward [lawn] Plan."

a rock-crushing plant speeds up progress

huge pipes drain water away from swampy areas

blasting accidents kill at least one worker

ice-skaters are the first citizens to flock to the park

cartmen driving two-horse trucks bring in fresh soil

Winter 1860: visitors begin to arrive

rich New Yorkers compete to drive the most expensive carriage

The city starts by buying land.
The landowners—561 of them—are paid to move out,
but the tenants who rent houses get nothing. In Seneca Village,
the largest settlement to be cleared, about 1,600 black and Irish people are
driven out. Construction begins in 1856, providing 20,000 jobs for the
poor. Central Park will not open officially until 1873, but New Yorkers
gleefully invade its walks, lawns, and lakes long before the work is finished.

Separate drives and paths keep the carriages of the rich away from the poorer strollers.

the Ninth District Provost Marshall's office—the "draft building"—is in a remote part of the city

the Invalid Corps of disabled veterans (ex-soldiers) marches in to help the police

Hundreds of rioters hang one African American man from a tree and set his body on fire.

rioters pelt the veteran soldiers with stones until they turn away

women join in the beating of soldiers and the police

rebellious firemen of the Black Joke company lead the riot

NO DRAFT

NO DRAFT

rioters bang pots and pans like gongs

OFFICE OF THE PROVOST MARSHAL 9TH DISTRICT

Draft riots

July 13, 1863

Almost a century after it won independence, the United States is at war again—this time with itself. The North fights the South in bloody battles. Southern Confederate states rely on black slaves to grow crops. Northern Unionist states want slavery to end. In New York City, a lottery system chooses who should be drafted—sent off to fight in the Unionist army.

The draft is deeply unpopular, especially among New York's many Irish workers. They do not want to fight. They are bitter that wealthy New Yorkers can avoid the draft by paying $300—more than a worker earns in a year. On a hot Monday in July 1863, their rage tears the city apart. They stone the office where the lottery is happening and set it on fire.

The draft protest turns into a race riot as the mob tortures and murders black New Yorkers. They see freed slaves as the cause of the war and as rivals for their poorly paid jobs. The riot continues for three days, until rain cools the sweltering streets and soldiers take control. When it ends, about 120 New Yorkers lie dead, with a further 2,000 injured.

Six thousand soldiers end the riots, attacking the crowd with rifles, bayonets, and big guns.

crowd members break up paving stones and hurl the pieces at the windows

the rebellious firemen carry turpentine, which they use to set fire to the offices

Troops help 237 black orphan children escape after rioters attack and burn their orphanage.

BLACK JOKE

protestors cut the telegraph wires to prevent the police from sending for more help

NO DRAFT

the wealthy "$300 men" are spotted and attacked

the rioters come from factories and tenement slums nearby

protestors carry "NO DRAFT" signs

policemen are driven away by the rioters

NO DRAFT

New York City in 1863

N

Ninth District Provost Marshall's office

Central Park

Old Delaware settlement

Hudson River

East River

Brooklyn

City Hall

Broadway

23

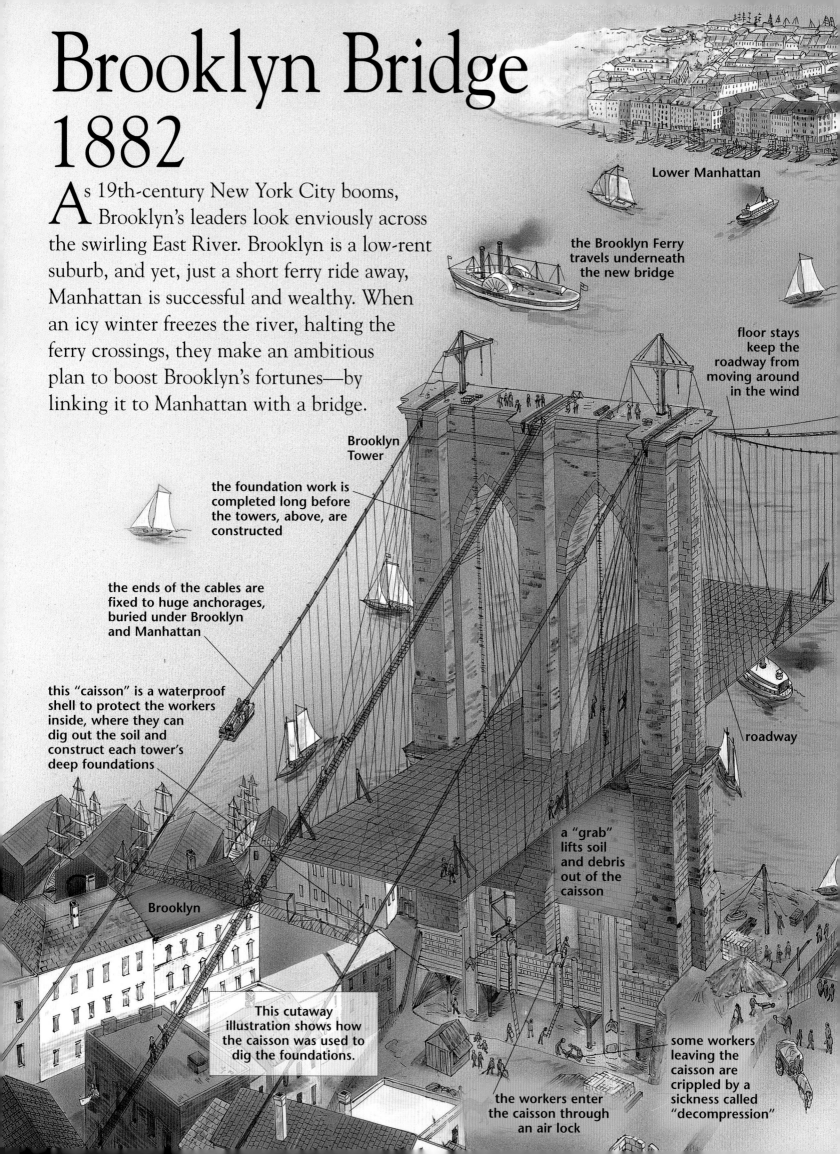

Brooklyn Bridge 1882

As 19th-century New York City booms, Brooklyn's leaders look enviously across the swirling East River. Brooklyn is a low-rent suburb, and yet, just a short ferry ride away, Manhattan is successful and wealthy. When an icy winter freezes the river, halting the ferry crossings, they make an ambitious plan to boost Brooklyn's fortunes—by linking it to Manhattan with a bridge.

Lower Manhattan

the Brooklyn Ferry travels underneath the new bridge

floor stays keep the roadway from moving around in the wind

Brooklyn Tower

the foundation work is completed long before the towers, above, are constructed

the ends of the cables are fixed to huge anchorages, buried under Brooklyn and Manhattan

this "caisson" is a waterproof shell to protect the workers inside, where they can dig out the soil and construct each tower's deep foundations

roadway

a "grab" lifts soil and debris out of the caisson

Brooklyn

This cutaway illustration shows how the caisson was used to dig the foundations.

some workers leaving the caisson are crippled by a sickness called "decompression"

the workers enter the caisson through an air lock

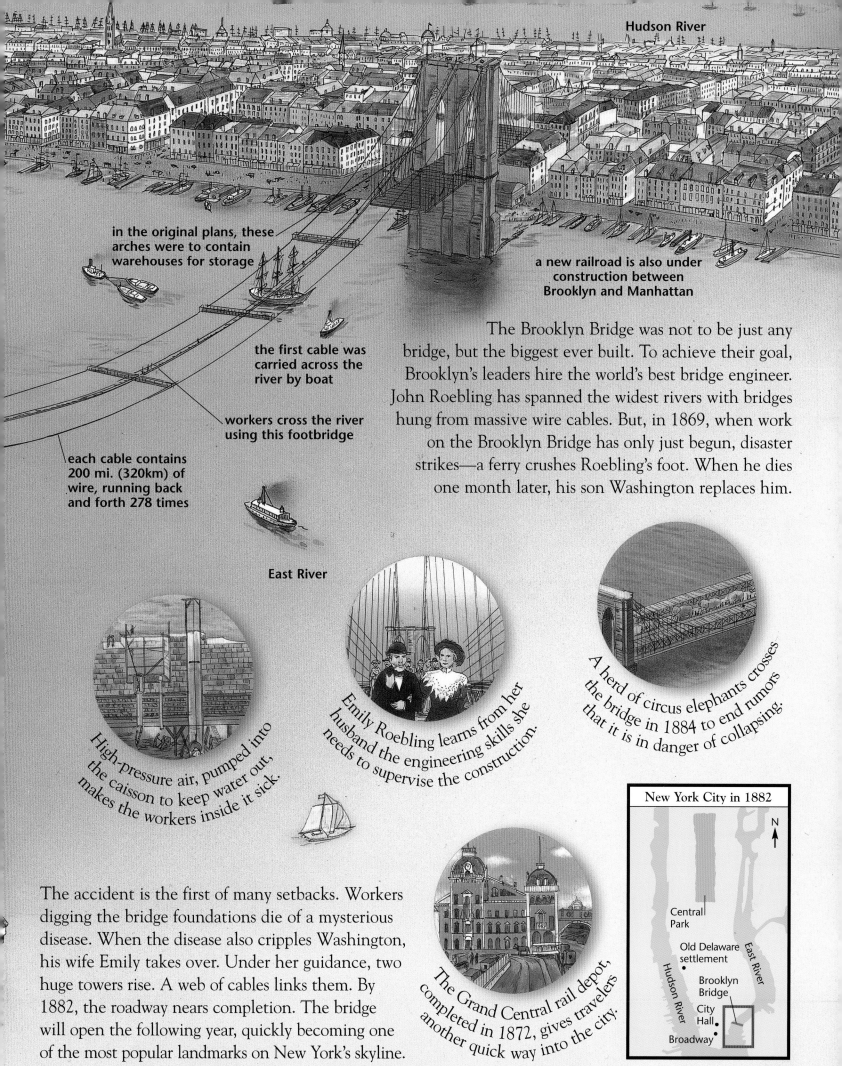

Hudson River

in the original plans, these arches were to contain warehouses for storage

the first cable was carried across the river by boat

workers cross the river using this footbridge

each cable contains 200 mi. (320km) of wire, running back and forth 278 times

East River

a new railroad is also under construction between Brooklyn and Manhattan

The Brooklyn Bridge was not to be just any bridge, but the biggest ever built. To achieve their goal, Brooklyn's leaders hire the world's best bridge engineer. John Roebling has spanned the widest rivers with bridges hung from massive wire cables. But, in 1869, when work on the Brooklyn Bridge has only just begun, disaster strikes—a ferry crushes Roebling's foot. When he dies one month later, his son Washington replaces him.

High-pressure air, pumped into the caisson to keep water out, makes the workers inside it sick.

Emily Roebling learns from her husband the engineering skills she needs to supervise the construction.

A herd of circus elephants crosses the bridge in 1884 to end rumors that it is in danger of collapsing.

The accident is the first of many setbacks. Workers digging the bridge foundations die of a mysterious disease. When the disease also cripples Washington, his wife Emily takes over. Under her guidance, two huge towers rise. A web of cables links them. By 1882, the roadway nears completion. The bridge will open the following year, quickly becoming one of the most popular landmarks on New York's skyline.

The Grand Central rail depot, completed in 1872, gives travelers another quick way into the city.

New York City in 1882

N

Central Park

Old Delaware settlement

Hudson River

East River

Brooklyn Bridge

City Hall

Broadway

Ellis Island 1906

Immigrants created the United States. They came to New York from Europe, seeking new lives or to escape persecution. By 1906, the number arriving each year has swelled to more than one million. For most, the first experience of their new homeland is on Ellis Island, in New York's harbor. Here they are tested, questioned, inspected, and sometimes rejected.

Crowded barges bring immigrants to Ellis Island from their big, trans-Atlantic liners, moored nearby.

Immigrants cross the Atlantic in the hot, noisy, dirty "steerage" cabins on board the ocean liners.

barges carry successful immigrants to Manhattan or New Jersey

bunk beds on chains lift up to the ceiling by day to make more space for new arrivals

the "Kissing Post" is a corridor where successful immigrants are reunited with their waiting relatives

in good weather, the medical inspections begin outside

a staircase leads up to the registry room, where the inspections take place

dormitory room

Sitting behind tall desks, immigration officials ask everyone exactly the same 29 questions.

metal pens keep people from each ship together

immigrants leave their heaviest luggage in a storeroom on the ground floor

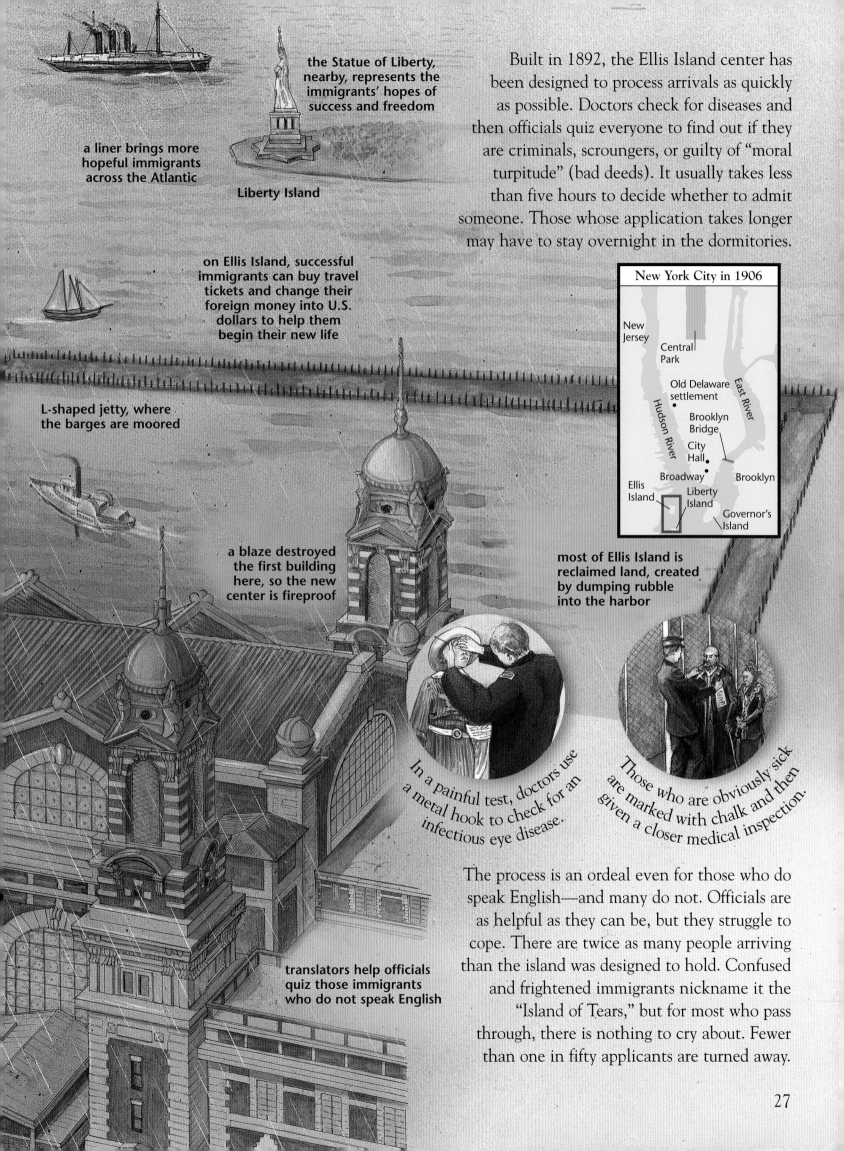

the Statue of Liberty, nearby, represents the immigrants' hopes of success and freedom

Liberty Island

a liner brings more hopeful immigrants across the Atlantic

Built in 1892, the Ellis Island center has been designed to process arrivals as quickly as possible. Doctors check for diseases and then officials quiz everyone to find out if they are criminals, scroungers, or guilty of "moral turpitude" (bad deeds). It usually takes less than five hours to decide whether to admit someone. Those whose application takes longer may have to stay overnight in the dormitories.

on Ellis Island, successful immigrants can buy travel tickets and change their foreign money into U.S. dollars to help them begin their new life

New York City in 1906

New Jersey
Central Park
Old Delaware settlement
Hudson River
Brooklyn Bridge
City Hall
Broadway
Ellis Island
Liberty Island
East River
Brooklyn
Governor's Island

L-shaped jetty, where the barges are moored

a blaze destroyed the first building here, so the new center is fireproof

most of Ellis Island is reclaimed land, created by dumping rubble into the harbor

In a painful test, doctors use a metal hook to check for an infectious eye disease.

Those who are obviously sick are marked with chalk and then given a closer medical inspection.

translators help officials quiz those immigrants who do not speak English

The process is an ordeal even for those who do speak English—and many do not. Officials are as helpful as they can be, but they struggle to cope. There are twice as many people arriving than the island was designed to hold. Confused and frightened immigrants nickname it the "Island of Tears," but for most who pass through, there is nothing to cry about. Fewer than one in fifty applicants are turned away.

Highs and lows 1930

to catch alcohol sellers by surprise, federal police officers raid a drinking club, or "speakeasy"—causing drinkers and dancing performers to flee

It is midnight in Harlem. In the Cotton Club, black musicians belt out hot jazz—for a white audience. "Prohibition" laws ban alcohol, but everyone is drinking it. The club's customers wear diamonds, yet outside there are people lining up for free soup. New York in the 1930s is a crazy mix of race, wealth, poverty, and crime.

Though slavery has ended, black and white Americans lead mostly separate lives. Music unites them. Harlem is Manhattan's black community, and rich white jazz lovers come here to see famous black musicians. Many people hate prohibition laws, and the club bribes the police to stay away. After a few drinks, it is easy to forget the squalor and troubles of the world outside.

a soup kitchen

costumes

homeless and out of work, many citizens are forced to line up for free food served at "soup kitchens"

city police officers inspect crates inside a truck to see if they contain alcoholic drinks for the club

New York City in 1930

N

The Bronx

Harlem River

Cotton Club

Harlem   East Harlem

Broadway

Central Park

Hudson River

East River

The police are tougher on black "speakeasies" (illegal bars) than on those where white people drink.

Harlem is a district of northern Manhattan, where a large community of African-Americans settled in the early 1900s

The Wall Street crash of 1929 is named after New York's financial district, where the crisis began.

But for the "down-and-outs" on the street, the main problem is survival. In 1929, the stock market on Wall Street went from boom to gloom. Many Americans had bet that the value of companies traded on the stock market would rise. Instead they fell, destroying banks, jobs, and life savings and beginning an economic depression that will last ten years. For its hungry victims, the Cotton Club is as far out of reach as the Moon.

28

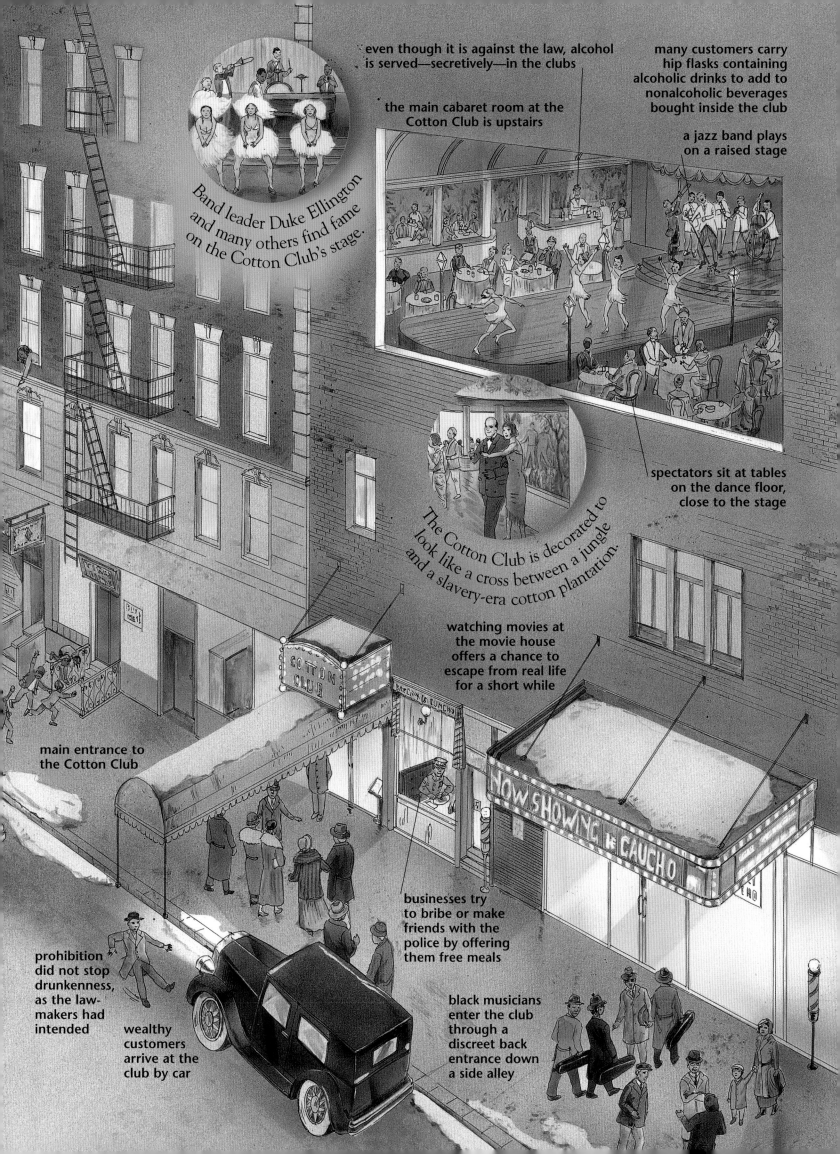

even though it is against the law, alcohol is served—secretively—in the clubs

many customers carry hip flasks containing alcoholic drinks to add to nonalcoholic beverages bought inside the club

the main cabaret room at the Cotton Club is upstairs

a jazz band plays on a raised stage

Band leader Duke Ellington and many others find fame on the Cotton Club's stage.

spectators sit at tables on the dance floor, close to the stage

The Cotton Club is decorated to look like a cross between a jungle and a slavery-era cotton plantation.

watching movies at the movie house offers a chance to escape from real life for a short while

main entrance to the Cotton Club

businesses try to bribe or make friends with the police by offering them free meals

prohibition did not stop drunkenness, as the law-makers had intended

wealthy customers arrive at the club by car

black musicians enter the club through a discreet back entrance down a side alley

COTTON CLUB

NOW SHOWING GAUCHO

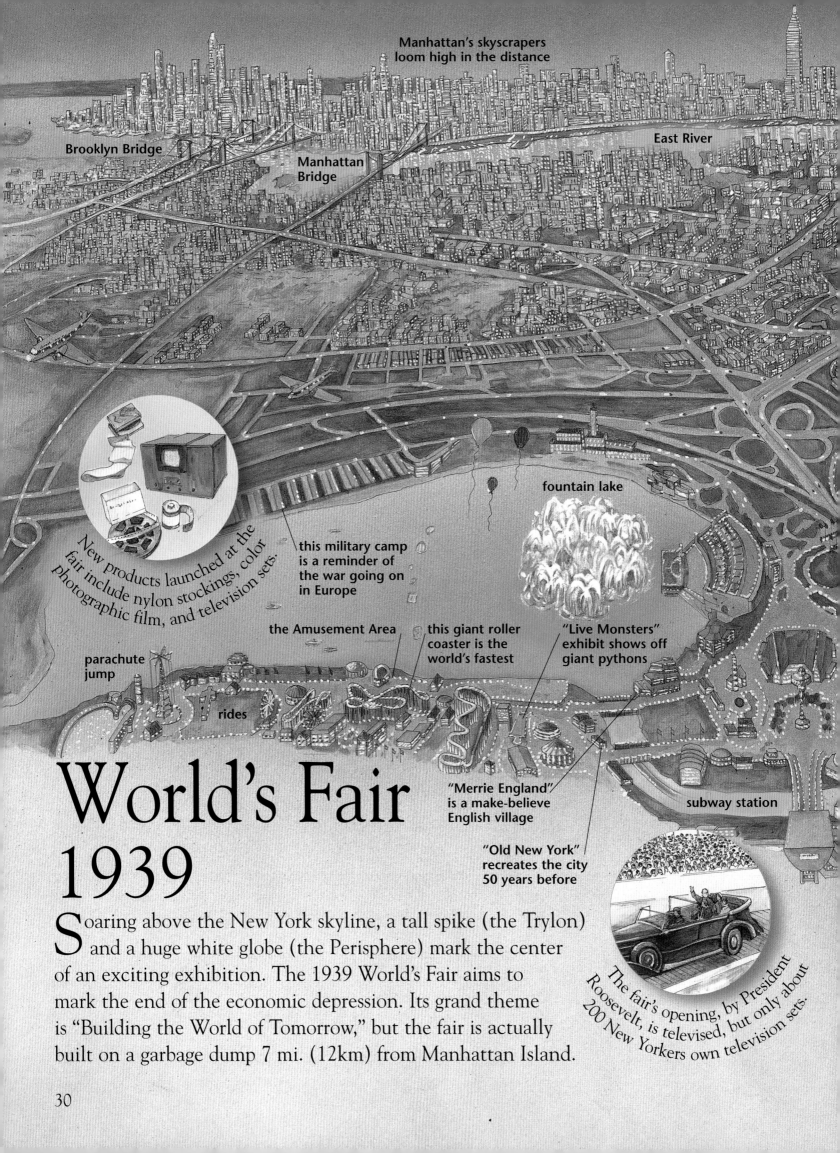

Manhattan's skyscrapers loom high in the distance

Brooklyn Bridge

Manhattan Bridge

East River

New products launched at the fair include nylon stockings, color photographic film, and television sets.

this military camp is a reminder of the war going on in Europe

fountain lake

the Amusement Area

this giant roller coaster is the world's fastest

"Live Monsters" exhibit shows off giant pythons

parachute jump

rides

"Merrie England" is a make-believe English village

subway station

"Old New York" recreates the city 50 years before

The fair's opening, by President Roosevelt, is televised, but only about 200 New Yorkers own television sets.

World's Fair 1939

Soaring above the New York skyline, a tall spike (the Trylon) and a huge white globe (the Perisphere) mark the center of an exciting exhibition. The 1939 World's Fair aims to mark the end of the economic depression. Its grand theme is "Building the World of Tomorrow," but the fair is actually built on a garbage dump 7 mi. (12km) from Manhattan Island.

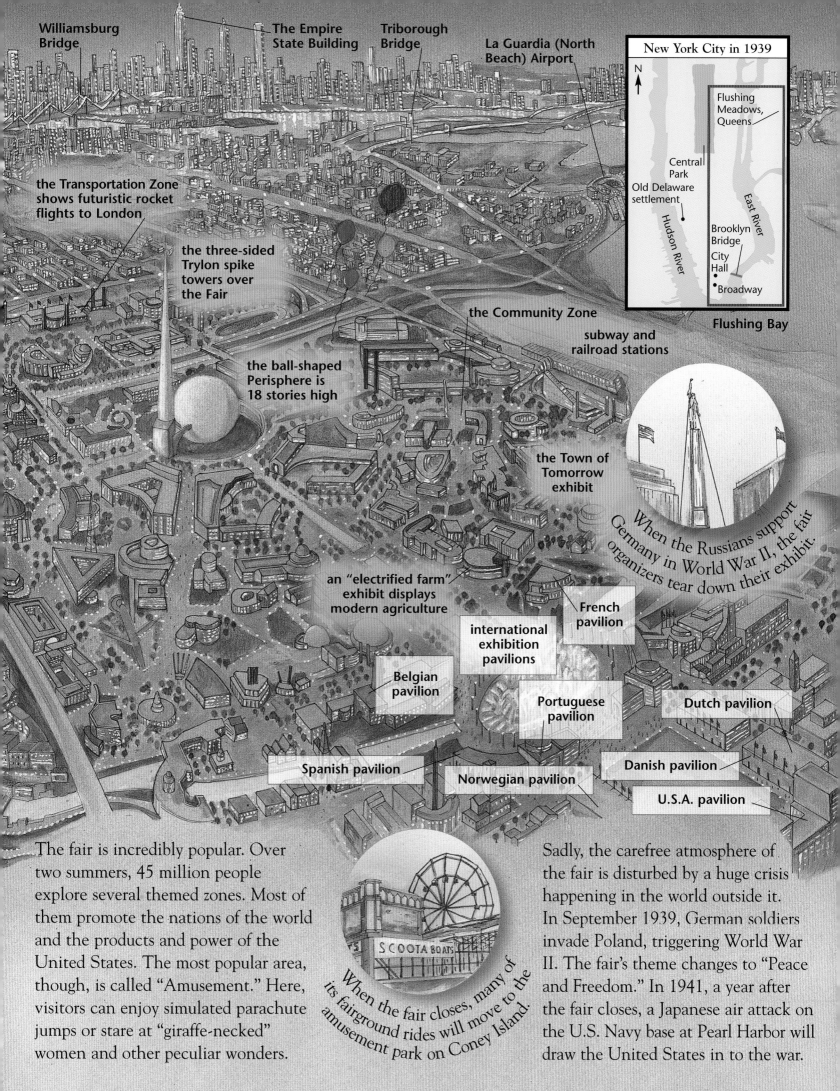

Williamsburg Bridge

The Empire State Building

Triborough Bridge

La Guardia (North Beach) Airport

New York City in 1939

N

Flushing Meadows, Queens

Central Park

Old Delaware settlement

Hudson River

East River

Brooklyn Bridge

City Hall

Broadway

Flushing Bay

the Transportation Zone shows futuristic rocket flights to London

the three-sided Trylon spike towers over the Fair

the Community Zone

subway and railroad stations

the ball-shaped Perisphere is 18 stories high

the Town of Tomorrow exhibit

When the Russians support Germany in World War II, the fair organizers tear down their exhibit.

an "electrified farm" exhibit displays modern agriculture

French pavilion

international exhibition pavilions

Belgian pavilion

Portuguese pavilion

Dutch pavilion

Spanish pavilion

Norwegian pavilion

Danish pavilion

U.S.A. pavilion

The fair is incredibly popular. Over two summers, 45 million people explore several themed zones. Most of them promote the nations of the world and the products and power of the United States. The most popular area, though, is called "Amusement." Here, visitors can enjoy simulated parachute jumps or stare at "giraffe-necked" women and other peculiar wonders.

SCOOTA BOATS

When the fair closes, many of its fairground rides will move to the amusement park on Coney Island.

Sadly, the carefree atmosphere of the fair is disturbed by a huge crisis happening in the world outside it. In September 1939, German soldiers invade Poland, triggering World War II. The fair's theme changes to "Peace and Freedom." In 1941, a year after the fair closes, a Japanese air attack on the U.S. Navy base at Pearl Harbor will draw the United States in to the war.

31

Pop and protest
April 15, 1967

As April drizzle drifts across New York's East River, it blows with it the sounds and smells of protest. There are rousing speeches, songs played on strummed guitars, and smoke from burning draft cards. For America is at war again, this time in Vietnam. And just as they did a century or so earlier, in 1863, New Yorkers are saying "We won't go!"

United Nations Headquarters, near the East River

In 1968, African-American civil rights campaigner Martin Luther King, Jr., will be assassinated by a gunman.

3,000 police officers patrol the march

the crowd fills Dag Hammarskjöld Plaza on East 47th Street

the protest organizers estimate that 400,000 people are marching from the park—it takes four hours for all of them to get out of the park

Martin Luther King, Jr. addresses the crowd

YANKEES COME HOME

United States troops have been in Vietnam since the 1950s. Their aim is to stop the spread of Communism. By 1967, 11,000 Americans and many more Vietnamese are dying each year. But the angry protesters gathering on East 47th Street do not fear the Communists. When civil rights leader Martin Luther King, Jr., shouts that the war is illegal and unjust, the huge crowd cheers in agreement.

The protesters marched here from Central Park, through the same streets where draft rioters fought troops in 1863. But today's protest is peaceful. It brings together young hippies, believers in peace, and older antiwar campaigners. In 1967, New York is a very different place. It is a center of culture and leads the world in pop music, beat poetry, and pop art.

New York City in 1967

N

United Nations buildings

Central Park

Old Delaware settlement

Hudson River

East River

Brooklyn Bridge

City Hall

Broadway

Pop-artist Andy Warhol has a studio overlooking the plaza where the antiwar marchers gather.

nearby, Andy Warhol's art studio overlooks the protest

musicians accompany the march with jazz, rock, and country music

power plant chimneys tower above the East River

drizzly April weather dampens the crowd

anti-Communists mingle in the crowd

about 100,000 people gather to hear Dr. King speak

slogans on protest signs criticize the war and the U.S. president

U.S. planes "carpet-bomb" huge areas of Vietnam at a time rather than aiming at specific targets.

supporters of the war throw eggs and red paint

a few protesters are bruised from fights with opponents—but only five people are arrested during the mostly peaceful protest

PEACE

BRING THEM HOME NOW

STOP THE DRAFT END THE WAR

GET OUT OF VIET NAM

BIG FIRM GET RICH IT'S DIG

NO VIETNAMESE EVER CALLED NIGGER

DRAFT KENNEDY

LOVE NOT WAR

THEY ARE MY BROTHER WHOM

By illegally burning their draft cards, the protesters show that they firmly refuse to go to war.

protest singer Phil Ochs waits to perform

the protest unites young and old, hippies and conservatives

barriers hold back the crowd

Return of the Apollo heroes

August 13, 1969

I t is summer in New York, but it seems to be snowing. New Yorkers are showering three space-age heroes in a paper blizzard—a "tickertape welcome." Heading the parade are astronauts Neil Armstrong, Buzz Aldrin, and Michael Collins. To get here, they traveled farther than anyone before them. Three weeks ago, the landing module of their *Apollo 11* spacecraft put two of them on the Moon.

two million New Yorkers watch the parade through the streets

New York City in 1969

N

Central Park

United Nations buildings

42nd St.

Old Delaware settlement

Hudson River

Brooklyn Bridge

City Hall

East River

Broadway

Armstrong and Aldrin planting an American flag on the lunar surface. The U.S. has truly won the Moon race.

Under construction nearby are the two towers of the World Trade Center—the world's tallest buildings.

motorcycle cops escort the astronauts for their safety

Apollo 11 is a triumph because it means that the U.S. has won the Space Race. The race began 12 years earlier, when America's bitter rival, the Soviet Union (Russia), launched Earth's first artificial satellite, *Sputnik*. The race got faster in 1961, when a Russian became the first human in space. A month after that, the U.S. president vowed that an American would land on the Moon by 1970.

office workers hang out of the highest windows

the route of the parade takes it right through Manhattan and Queens

the crowd showers the parade with every kind of paper scraps

the cars following behind carry the astronauts' families

journalists will beam the story worldwide

Neil Armstrong, Apollo 11 Mission Commander

Michael Collins, Command Module Pilot

A tickertape parade will soon reward the New York Mets baseball team for winning the World Series.

Many New Yorkers skip the parade to go to the Woodstock rock festival, happening 80 mi. (130km) away.

Buzz Aldrin, Lunar Module Pilot

John Lindsay, mayor of New York City

Thomas Paine, head of NASA

the cars head down 42nd Street to the United Nations Headquarters for a special medal presentation

later, the U.S. president's private plane takes the astronauts on to Chicago, Illinois

Armstrong, Aldrin, and Collins have done it—with just months to spare. Yet the three astronauts are bewildered. Years of training gave them the skills they needed to reach the Moon and land on it. But nobody taught them how to be heroes. Ears ringing from all the cheering, they drive to a glitzy reception at the United Nations building—and then on to a whirlwind tour of the world.

Times Square
December 31, 1975

New Yorkers have gone wild! They have crammed into the sleazy, dirty, dangerous Times Square and waited for hours in the winter rain. They have come here on December 31 to celebrate the end of 1975. Now, at 11:59 P.M., all their eyes are on the ball of light that is dropping to signal midnight. At least for tonight, they can forget their troubles and hope for a better New Year ahead.

They have plenty to forget. New York is in a desperate place. The city council is broke and can hardly pay its employees' wages. The streets are rundown, vandalized, and covered in graffiti and rotting garbage. Amid the decay, New York has become America's capital of crime. And of all the city's mean streets, Times Square is the meanest of all.

70,000 tons of trash litters the streets in December 1975 after garbage workers go on strike.

New York City in 1975

N

- Central Park
- Times Square
- Old Delaware settlement
- East River
- Brooklyn Bridge
- City Hall
- Broadway
- Hudson River

When power fails for 24 hours in the summer of 1977, looters and rioters run wild in the dark.

the aluminum ball weighs 100 lbs. (45kg)

the falling of the time ball marks midnight—it takes one full minute to fall

Times Square's neon signs are famous

the building is named after The New York Times newspaper, which was based here until 1914

the Times Building, at 1 Times Square

the Times Building was the second-tallest in the world when it was built

The fortunes of the city improve, though not in 1976. The following year, the people elect a new mayor, Ed Koch. Pushy and plainspoken, he puts New York's finances back on track. He starts schemes to stop crime and improve the streets. So when the ball drops to mark the end of the 1970s, it will be above a cleaner, safer, glitzier Times Square.

shops have boarded-up windows in case of crowd trouble or looting

freezing-cold rain soaks the revelers

Spray-painted graffiti covers subway trains and mark the territory, or "turf," of rival gangs.

New York City's theaters cluster around busy Times Square

the crowd is smaller than usual because people are saving money and staying at home

the neighborhood is home to drifters and the homeless

pickpockets (thieves) prey on the crowd unnoticed

Ed Koch is elected as Mayor of New York City in 1977 and serves in office from 1978 until 1989.

an electronic "zipper" on the Times Building shows up-to-date world news

TIMES SQUARE BOWLING

Ground Zero

September 11, 2001

Early on a September morning, a soaring airliner slams through one of New York's tallest skyscrapers. At first, it looks like a tragic, terrible accident. Then 17 minutes later, a second plane hits the other tower of the World Trade Center. Now the truth is horribly clear. The United States is under attack. Extremist Islamic terrorists, seizing control of the planes, have used the aircraft as deadly weapons.

Jet fuel in the aircraft catches fire as the planes crash, creating searing fireballs that burn through the towers.

the crushed concrete creates giant dust clouds that blanket Manhattan

the attack cuts power to many buildings in the neighborhood

live television coverage of the disaster continues all around the world for days after the attacks

hidden tanks of fuel and air-conditioning coolants, once part of the buildings, are an explosion hazard

fires still burn beneath the rubble

Vesey Street

The impacts, and the fireballs they create, shock and terrify New York's citizens and visitors. The city's emergency workers remain calm, though. Dodging stumbling victims in dust-filled streets, firefighters and medical teams race to the twin towers. Many of them are among those killed in the attacks—almost 3,000 people—when the buildings fall to the ground midmorning.

North Tower wreckage

History's worst terrorist attack may have happened in New York City, but the whole world feels its impact. As rescuers search the wreckage, U.S. president George W. Bush vows to hunt down those who plotted the suicide attacks. He unleashes a "War on Terror." His target is the terrorist group al-Qaeda and its supporters in Iraq, Afghanistan, and beyond. This war continues today.

New York City in 2001

N

Times Square and 42nd Street

Old Delaware settlement

Manhattan Island

East River

Site of the World Trade Center

Brooklyn Bridge

Hudson River

City Hall

Broadway

Most of those who die when the towers collapse are above the floors where the planes strike.

three more buildings within the World Trade Center complex are damaged beyond repair

rescuers call the site "Ground Zero"—the name given to places where atomic bombs were dropped at the end of World War II (1939–1945)

building materials continue to fall, endangering rescuers

Church Street

Firefighters raise American flags on the rubble to remember the victims and defy their killers.

the 110-floor towers collapse into piles of rubble hardly taller than a house

Liberty Street

South Tower wreckage

some victims survive being buried in the rubble for 24 hours

emergency medical teams begin treating victims within seven minutes of the first attack

West Street

400 rescue dogs help search through the rubble

half of New York's firefighters arrive at the scene very quickly

On each anniversary of the attacks, twin banks of powerful lamps will recreate the fallen towers.

39

Modern NYC Today

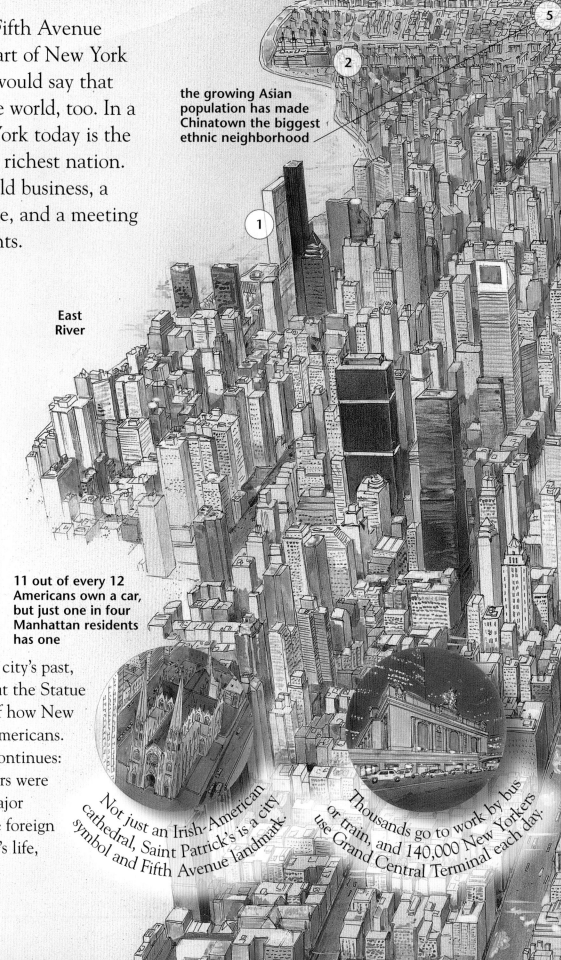

Stand on Manhattan's Fifth Avenue and you are at the heart of New York City. Proud New Yorkers would say that you are at the center of the world, too. In a way, they are right. New York today is the greatest city of the world's richest nation. It is a marketplace for world business, a crossroads for world culture, and a meeting place for world governments.

KEY to buildings and districts:

1   United Nations Headquarters
2   Peter Cooper Village
    and Stuyvesant Town
3   Brooklyn
4   Brooklyn Bridge
5   Chinatown
6   Chrysler Building
7   The Statue of Liberty
8   Business district
9   Site of World Trade Center
10 Five Points
11 Washington Square
12 Greenwich Village
13 Garment District
14 Empire State Building
15 New York Public Library
16 Times Square
17 Saint Patrick's Cathedral
18 Rockefeller Center
19 Fifth Avenue
    (running north to south)
20 Central Park East

New Yorkers are proud of their city's past, too. They are quick to point out the Statue of Liberty, a lasting reminder of how New York welcomed hopeful new Americans. And the immigrant tradition continues: one-third of today's New Yorkers were born abroad. All the world's major languages are spoken here. The foreign faces and voices renew the city's life, culture, and boundless energy.

Brooklyn, like Manhattan, is one of New York's Five Boroughs—the other three are Queens, the Bronx, and Staten Island

the growing Asian population has made Chinatown the biggest ethnic neighborhood

East River

11 out of every 12 Americans own a car, but just one in four Manhattan residents has one

Not just an Irish-American cathedral, Saint Patrick's is a city symbol and Fifth Avenue landmark.

Thousands go to work by bus or train, and 140,000 New Yorkers use Grand Central Terminal each day.

old Dutch New York is now the business district

in bustling Midtown Manhattan, 100-year-old skyscrapers still stand among new towers

7

8

9

10

11

12

13

14

15

16

17

18

19

Hudson River

New York will need all the energy it can get because it faces a difficult future. Its businesses and its people are short of money. In the future, the planet's rising oceans may threaten to swamp this sea-level city. Yet New York has fought off disaster before. It has survived wars, fires, terrorism, financial collapse, and crime waves. A century from now it will surely be as big, bold, and brash as ever.

New York City in 2010

N

Central Park

Old Delaware settlement

Brooklyn Bridge

City Hall

Broadway

Hudson River

East River

more than half of all New Yorkers use public transportation to get to work

some of the world's most expensive apartments overlook Central Park from Fifth Avenue

20

Central Park

the Arsenal Art Gallery

The Empire State Building was the city's tallest until 1972, when the World Trade Center was built.

Glossary

Words in *italics* refer to other glossary entries.

al-Qaeda
A terrorist organization, whose members aim violent attacks at those they believe oppose *Islam*.

ancestor
Someone's parents, and also their grandparents, great-grandparents, and so on, through to the oldest members of a family.

Apollo 11
An American space mission that succeeded in landing two astronauts, Neil Armstrong and Edwin "Buzz" Aldrin, on the Moon in July 1969. A third astronaut, Michael Collins, piloted the *Apollo 11* Command Module and remained in orbit around the Moon while Armstrong and Aldrin walked on the lunar surface.

atomic bombs
Hugely powerful bombs that continue to cause sickness and death long after they explode.

barracks
Living accommodation for soldiers.

Broadway
The oldest north-to-south street in *Manhattan*, running the entire length of the island.

a Delaware woman tends to a fruit crop in a small garden

brownstone
A style of house, popular in the 1800s, named after the brown sandstone used to build it.

Bush, George W. (born 1946)
The 43rd president of the United States, serving as president between 2001 and 2009.

cannon
A heavy, wheeled gun that fires large shells or cannonballs.

Castle Clinton
A large stone fort built in 1811 to protect the southern tip of *Manhattan*.

a Canada goose flying above Manhattan

chandler
Originally candlemakers, chandlers at ports sell the hardware that ships need for sailing and repairs.

Charles II (1630–1685)
English king during whose reign England seized control of New Netherland from the Dutch.

City Hall
The building in Lower *Manhattan* from which the mayor and city council govern New York.

civil war
A war between people of the same country.

colony
A settlement set up in a new land but still ruled from the settlers' homeland.

Communism
A way of organizing a country so that its people govern themselves and share the country's wealth.

Coney Island
Originally an island on the southern Atlantic coast of Brooklyn, now joined to it by reclaimed land.

Confederacy
The group of Southern states that left the United States between 1861 and 1865, triggering a *civil war* over the right to own slaves.

cooper
A worker who makes wooden barrels.

Maryland soldiers are on the charge at Brooklyn Heights in 1776, during the American Revolution.

Delaware
Native American people, also known as the Lenape, who lived in New York and New Jersey until European settlers took the land from them.

Declaration of Independence
The document signed by leaders of the American *colonies* in 1776 by which they refused to be governed by Great Britain any longer.

decompression sickness
A crippling and sometimes deadly disease suffered by people who work underground or underwater in compressed air.

Delaware fishermen using baskets to scoop up oysters

Downing, Andrew (1815–1852)
A landscape architect who suggested the creation of Central Park in *Manhattan*.

draft
An order forcing people to fight in a war.

Duke of York (1633–1701)
James Stuart, brother of England's king *Charles II*, who gave his name to New York and who later became king of England, Scotland, and Ireland.

Ellington, Duke (1899–1974)
A famous African-American composer, musician, and band leader who helped win respect for jazz as a serious and important style of music.

ethnic
Belonging to a group whose members maintain traditional customs, often belonging to an *immigrant* group or having *ancestors* who were *immigrants*.

exhibit
Something put on display.

export
Something sent out of a country for sale abroad.

fort
An area protected from attack by high, strong walls.

fortified town
A town surrounded by defensive walls.

frigate
A three-masted sailing warship, with up to 36 cannons on board.

fusillade
In a battle, the firing of a large number of small guns, such as rifles and pistols, all at once.

game
Wild birds and animals hunted for food.

governor
A government officer who controls a *colony* or state.

Ground Zero
A name given to places where *atomic bombs* were dropped at the end of *World War II*, as well as to sites of terrible destruction.

Hudson, Henry (died 1611)
English sailor and navigator who, in 1609, explored New York Harbor for his Dutch masters.

immigrant
Someone who leaves their homeland behind and comes to a different country to start a new life.

Islam
The religion of Muslims, who worship one god and believe that Muhammad (c. 570?–632) was his prophet (a communicator of the god's will).

King, Martin Luther, Jr. (1929–1968)
firemen of the Black Joke company leading a riot in New York City in July 1863
An African-American Christian leader who campaigned for equal rights for black people.

Koch, Ed (born 1924)
Politician who, as mayor of New York City from 1978 to 1989, helped rescue the city from decay and financial ruin.

Manahatouh
The *Delaware* name for *Manhattan* Island.

Manhattan
The long, narrow island at the center of New York City between the Hudson and East rivers.

Maryland
Originally an English colony on the Atlantic coast, southwest of New York. It is now an American state.

the Statue of Liberty

mercenary
A professional soldier who fights for anyone who will pay him or her.

merchant
Someone who buys and sells things.

migrant
Someone who moves from one region to make their home in another.

musket
An old-fashioned gun with a long barrel, fired from the shoulder like a rifle.

Native Americans
People who lived in America before the continent was settled by Europeans in the 1500s.

Pearl Harbor
A U.S. Navy base in Hawaii attacked in 1941 by Japan, thereby drawing the United States in to *World War II*.

persecution
The bad treatment of a person or group of people, often for reasons of religious or political belief.

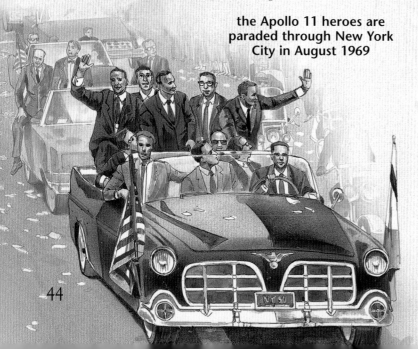
the Apollo 11 heroes are paraded through New York City in August 1969

plantation
A large farm estate in a *colony*, often worked by slave labor.

pop art
A style of art from the 1960s using strong colors and bold images, often based on advertising, news, or photographic images.

prohibition
A law introduced in the United States in 1920 that banned the sale of alcoholic drinks.

Queens
The largest of New York's five boroughs, to the east of Brooklyn and southeast of Upper *Manhattan*.

ramparts
Protected walkways on top of the walls of a castle or fortress.

antiwar protesters

rigging
Ropes used to support and control the masts, yards, and sails of a ship.

Roebling, John (1806–1869)
German-American engineer who designed the Brooklyn Bridge.

Roosevelt, Franklin Delano (1882–1945)
New York governor and 32nd U.S. president, "FDR" guided the country back to work and wealth after the *Wall Street crash of 1929*.

settler
Someone who travels with others to a distant, often empty land to make it their home.

snuff
Powdered tobacco, taken by sniffing it up the nose.

soup kitchen
A city-street kitchen serving free food to the poor during times of economic depression.

Space Race
The competition in the 1960s between the U.S. and the U.S.S.R. to land astronauts on the Moon.

speakeasy
An unlawful bar secretly serving alcohol during Prohibition in the United States.

Statue of Liberty
A colossal statue in New York Harbor, presented to the city by the French people in 1886 to thank Americans for welcoming so many European immigrants.

stock exchange or stock market
A place where traders gamble on the future value of businesses and by doing so raise money for the expansion of those businesses. Traders win or lose money by betting on the price of stocks—tokens representing the value of companies.

stockade
A crude fort, made by hammering wooden stakes into the ground around an area at risk of attack.

Stuyvesant, Peter (c. 1610–1672)
Governor of the Dutch colony on *Manhattan* that became New York when he surrendered to Great Britain in 1664.

suicide attack
A *terrorist* attack that the attacker does not expect to survive.

telegraph wires
Cables used in a signaling system that sends letters in a code of electric pulses.

terrorist
Someone who seeks power by frightening others with acts or threats of violence and crime.

Times Square
A large square where *Broadway* meets Seventh Avenue, in the heart of New York's theater district, in Midtown *Manhattan*.

twin towers
The tallest pair of buildings in the *World Trade Center*, destroyed in 2001 by a *terrorist* attack.

Union
The Northern states that opposed slavery and fought a *civil war* between 1861 and 1865 against the *Confederacy*, which favored it.

the Brooklyn Bridge under construction

United Nations
An organization, started in 1945 and based in New York, in which the world's countries meet to promote peace.

Wall Street crash of 1929
A disastrous financial collapse of the New York stock market, named after the street on which it is located.

War on Terror
The campaign by the United States and its allies to try to stop *terrorism* after the 2001 attacks that destroyed the *twin towers* of the *World Trade Center*.

Warhol, Andy (1928–1987)
An American artist who, in the 1960s, was a founder of the *pop art* movement in New York.

Washington, George (1732–1799)
America's first president, whose defeat in the 1776 Battle of Brooklyn allowed British troops to capture New York.

World Trade Center
A complex of office buildings in Lower *Manhattan* which was destroyed in a 2001 *terrorist* attack.

World War II (1939–1945)
A catastrophic six-year war in which Great Britain, the United States, and their military allies fought an alliance that included Germany, Italy, and Japan.

World's Fair
A giant exhibition held in New York in 1939 in which many countries showed off their proudest industrial and scientific achievements.

Index

the Manhattan skyline, as seen from the New York borough of Queens, in 1939

KINGFISHER
LONDON & NEW YORK

Copyright © Kingfisher 2010

Published in the United States by Kingfisher,
175 Fifth Ave., New York, NY 10010
Kingfisher is an imprint of Macmillan Children's Books, London.
All rights reserved.

Consultant: Eric Homberger, Emeritus Professor,
Department of American Studies, University of East Anglia, U.K.

Additional illustration work by Monica Favilli and Cecilia Scutti

Distributed in the U.S. by Macmillan, 175 Fifth Ave., New York, NY 10010
Distributed in Canada by H.B. Fenn and Company Ltd.,
34 Nixon Road, Bolton, Ontario L7E 1W2

Library of Congress Cataloging-in-Publication data has been applied for.

ISBN 978-0-7534-6416-8

Kingfisher books are available for special promotions and premiums.
For details contact: Special Markets Department, Macmillan,
175 Fifth Avenue, New York, NY 10010.

For more information, please visit www.kingfisherpublications.com

Printed in Taiwan
10 9 8 7 6 5 4 3 2 1
1TR/0310/SHENS/CLSN/157MA/C

In the early 1800s, the Brooklyn area is nothing more than a collection of scattered towns.